LOVE'S ENCHANTED WHISPERS

LOVE'S ENCHANTED WHISPERS

JOEL HAWKSLEY

J & Washington Network

CONTENTS

Dedication ix

Forward xi

Warning: Love's Crack xiii

PART I
THE AWAKENING OF LOVE 1

1 First Glance 2

2 Stolen Glances 3

3 Sweet Serenade 4

4 Whispered Secrets 5

5 Hidden Yearnings 6

PART II
PASSION'S EMBRACE 7

6 Fire and Flame 8

7 Silken Touch 9

8 Ecstasy's Dance 10

9 Breathless Moments 11

10 Entwined 12

PART III

THE DEPTHS OF DESIRE   13

11 Velvet Nights   14

12 Forbidden Longings   15

13 Temptation's Call   16

14 Moonlit Rendezvous   17

15 Eternal Flames   18

PART IV
TRIALS OF THE HEART   19

16 Stormy Seas   20

17 Whispers of Doubt   21

18 Love's Labyrinth   22

19 Shattered Trust   23

20 Hearts Repaired   24

PART V
SACRED UNION   25

21 Vows Unbroken   26

22 Sacred Bond   27

23 Eternal Embrace   28

24 Union of Souls   29

25 Love's Sanctuary   30

PART VI
LOVE'S ETERNAL DANCE   31

26 Timeless Waltz   32

27 Celestial Dance   33

28 Eternal Tango 34

29 Moonlight Ballet 35

30 Dance of Forever 36

PART VII
SEASONS OF INTIMACY 37

31 Spring's Embrace 38

32 Summer's Heat 39

33 Autumn's Whisper 40

34 Winter's Warmth 41

35 Seasons' Cycle 42

PART VIII
LOVE'S ETERNAL ECHO 43

36 Whispered Memories 44

37 Timeless Reverie 45

38 Echoes of the Heart 46

39 Eternal Reflection 47

40 Forever's Echo 48

PART IX
THE EPHEMERAL AND THE ETERNAL 49

41 Fleeting Moments 50

42 Eternal Flame 51

43 Passing Shadows 52

44 Timeless Love 53

45 Eternal Echo 54

PART X
REFLECTIONS AND REVERIES

46   Mirror of the Heart   56

47   Dreams of Yesterday   57

48   Reflections in the Moonlight   58

49   Reverie of the Stars   59

50   Reflections of Forever   60

Epilogue   61
Appendices   63
Glossary of Terms   67
About The Author   71

Dedication

To all those who love, all those who have loved, and all those who will love,

This collection is dedicated to you. At 57 years of age, I have witnessed love take on myriad forms, each one a unique and precious manifestation of the human spirit. Love is not confined by time, space, or circumstance; it is an ever-present force that shapes and defines our existence.

To truly know love, one must begin by loving oneself. Only through self-acceptance and self-compassion can we extend our hearts fully to those around us. It is in this act of self-love that we find the strength and courage to love others deeply and unconditionally.

May these poems be a reflection of the love that binds us all, a testament to the power of intimacy and connection. Let them remind you of the beauty of loving and being loved, and inspire you to cherish the love that you hold within and share with the world.

With heartfelt gratitude and hope,
Joel Hawksley

Welcome to "Love's Enchanted Whispers: Fifty Exotic Poems of Intimacy," a collection that beckons you to embark on a journey through the many facets of love. Within these pages, you'll find yourself immersed in a world where the elegance of Shakespearean expression meets the accessibility of modern English, crafting an experience that is both timeless and profoundly relatable.

Love, in all its forms, is the universal thread that binds us together. Whether you're experiencing the rush of a new romance, the deep connection of a long-term partnership, or the bittersweet nuances of a love lost and found, these poems are written to resonate with your heart. They speak to the yearning glances, the whispered secrets, the passionate embraces, and the silent reflections that define our most intimate relationships.

Each poem in this collection is a dance of words, designed to evoke the rich array of emotions that accompany love and intimacy. From the tender beginnings of infatuation to the fiery depths of desire, and from the trials that test our bonds to the serene comfort of enduring love, these verses invite you to explore the full spectrum of romantic experience.

As you read, allow yourself to be transported by the lyrical beauty and evocative imagery. Let the rhythms and cadences of these poems awaken your senses and stir your soul. Whether you're seeking to rekindle the flame of an existing love or yearning to experience the magic of romance anew, this collection offers a sanctuary of passion and connection.

Love is an eternal theme, one that transcends time and place. By blending the timeless style of William Shakespeare with the nuances of contemporary language, I aim to create a bridge that connects the past with the present, offering a fresh perspective on the ageless dance of love.

I invite you to lose yourself in these pages, to savor each line, and to let the enchantment of love's whispers guide you. May these poems inspire you to cherish the love you have, seek the love you desire, and embrace the profound beauty of loving and being loved.

With heartfelt passion,

Joel Hawksley

WARNING: LOVE'S CRACK

In love's tender sprout, a fragile seed,
Lies a heart's hope, a delicate creed,
But beware the cracks that subtly weave,
Through passion's soil, they silently cleave.

Doubt's whisper, a shadow in the mind,
Seeds of mistrust, in corners confined,
It spreads like a vine, consuming light,
Turning day to an endless night.

Pride, a barrier that stands so tall,
A wall of ego, destined to fall,
It divides the hearts that once beat as one,
Leaving love's garden bleak and undone.

Neglect, a silent thief in the dark,
Stealing joy with a careless remark,
Time forgotten, moments slipped away,
Turning vibrant hues to shades of gray.

Betrayal's dagger, sharp and cold,
A wound that festers, bitter and bold,
Its scar remains, a painful trace,
Marring love's once-beautiful face.

Jealousy's fire, burning bright,
Consuming trust in its fervent light,
It blinds the eyes to love's pure intent,
Leaving ashes where hearts once were spent.

Lies, the cracks that undermine,
Trust erodes, line by line,
Truth, the glue that holds hearts close,
In its absence, love's death it will host.

So tend to love with gentle care,
Beware the cracks that lie hidden there,
For in vigilance and in truth's embrace,
Love can flourish, time's trials efface.

The Awakening of Love

First Glance

In a crowded room where strangers drift and sway,
My eyes caught thine and all the world did fade,
A spark ignited, night turned into day,
And in that moment, love's first steps were made.

Thy gaze a beacon, piercing through the din,
A silent promise whispered through the air,
In that brief instant, heart and soul akin,
We found a bond so deep, beyond compare.

Oh, fleeting glance, a prelude to our tale,
Where destinies entwine in fateful dance,
Two souls adrift on love's eternal gale,
United by a single, stolen glance.

Thus, in that crowded room, our hearts aligned,
A love awakened by our eyes combined.

CHAPTER 2

Stolen Glances

Amidst the throng, where shadows softly blend,
Our eyes did meet, a secret left untold,
With every glance, our spirits seek to send
A message woven pure, in threads of gold.

Through veils of silence, passion's fire did spark,
Unspoken words exchanged in fleeting looks,
A hidden language kindled in the dark,
With chapters written, though no page in books.

Each stolen glance a bridge across the space,
Where lovers' hearts converge in sweet embrace,
In crowded realms, where time itself does race,
We find our haven in each other's face.

Thus, through the night, our secret love takes flight,
In stolen glances, burning ever bright.

CHAPTER 3

Sweet Serenade

Beneath the moon's soft glow, thy song did play,
A melody that danced upon the breeze,
Each note a whisper, chasing night away,
A serenade to set my heart at ease.

Thy voice, a silken thread that binds me tight,
In harmony, our souls begin to weave,
A lullaby that drifts through starry night,
In every breath, a promise to believe.

Oh, how thy song does waken dreams untold,
In lilting strains, my spirit takes to flight,
A symphony of love that makes me bold,
In echoes sweet, we banish dark of night.

So sing, my love, and let the music flow,
In sweet serenade, our hearts aglow.

CHAPTER 4

Whispered Secrets

In shadowed alcoves, hidden from the light,
Our whispered secrets softly intertwine,
With every breath, our souls take wing in flight,
A sacred bond, our love's unspoken sign.

Thy voice, a murmur in the quiet dark,
Confessions born of passion's gentle flame,
In hushed exchanges, hearts do leave their mark,
As whispered secrets set our love aflame.

Each word a promise, fragile yet so strong,
A vow unbroken in the still of night,
In secret whispers, where we both belong,
We find our truth, our love's enduring light.

Thus, in the quiet, where our secrets play,
Our whispered love does guide us on our way.

CHAPTER 5

Hidden Yearnings

Beneath the surface, where desires dwell,
Our hidden yearnings simmer, wild and free,
In silent moments, where our glances tell,
Of passions deep as any boundless sea.

Thy touch, a ghost upon my willing skin,
A phantom ache that echoes in the night,
In every breath, our secret dreams begin,
As hidden yearnings set our souls alight.

Oh, how we yearn, in shadows and in light,
For tender caress and whispered sighs,
In longing looks that pierce the velvet night,
Our silent pleas, our unspoken cries.

Thus, in the depths where hidden yearnings lie,
Our hearts converge beneath love's midnight sky.

PART II

Passion's Embrace

CHAPTER 6

Fire and Flame

In love's embrace, where passions freely blaze,
Our hearts ignite with fervor's wild delight,
A burning fire, unquenched by time or days,
As embers spark beneath the starry night.

Thy touch, a flame that sears my willing soul,
In every caress, the fire grows anew,
Our love a pyre, impossible to control,
Consuming all, yet leaving us so true.

We dance amidst the flames, entwined and free,
A symphony of heat and wild desire,
In passion's arms, we find our destiny,
Our souls alight in love's eternal fire.

Thus, in this blaze, where fire and flame conspire,
Our hearts are forged in love's unending fire.

CHAPTER 7

Silken Touch

Thy silken touch, a whisper on my skin,
A tender brush that sends my spirit high,
In every stroke, our love does thus begin,
A gentle breath, a soft and longing sigh.

Each caress, a symphony so sweet,
Where fingertips compose a lover's song,
In silken touch, our bodies' pulses beat,
Creating harmony where we belong.

Thy hands, a poet's quill upon my flesh,
In every line, a tale of passion penned,
We weave a story, vivid and afresh,
In silken touch, where love and bodies blend.

Thus, in the night, where silken touches play,
Our hearts and souls do dance till break of day.

CHAPTER 8

Ecstasy's Dance

In ecstasy's dance, where bodies intertwine,
We move as one, in rhythm's sweet embrace,
Our hearts in sync, our spirits all align,
As passion's beat sets forth our wondrous chase.

Thy movements guide, a maestro of delight,
In every step, we find our love's refrain,
A waltz of whispers, tender in the night,
As ecstasy's dance erases every pain.

Our bodies speak in language pure and true,
In every touch, a thousand words convey,
We lose ourselves in love's enchanting view,
As ecstasy's dance leads us far away.

Thus, in this dance, where ecstasy holds sway,
Our hearts and souls in perfect time do sway.

Breathless Moments

In breathless moments, just before the kiss,
The world falls silent, time itself stands still,
A fleeting pause, a prelude to our bliss,
Where all is calm, yet charged with passion's thrill.

Thy breath, a whisper mingled close with mine,
In that brief instant, love's pure essence found,
A tender sigh, a touch of the divine,
Where heartbeats echo in a silent sound.

Oh, how we linger in this sacred space,
A breathless moment, pregnant with desire,
In every pause, we find our love's embrace,
As time suspends within love's gentle fire.

Thus, in the stillness, where our breath does meet,
We find our heaven in a kiss so sweet.

CHAPTER 10

Entwined

In love's embrace, where two become but one,
Our bodies merge, entwined in passion's hold,
A sacred union, second to none,
In every touch, a story yet untold.

Thy limbs with mine, a seamless, perfect blend,
In close embrace, our hearts do beat as one,
A timeless dance, where lovers' souls transcend,
And all the world around us is undone.

Entwined in love, we find our purest truth,
A bond that strengthens with each passing day,
In passion's hold, we live our endless youth,
Our spirits joined, in love's eternal sway.

Thus, in this embrace, where we are entwined,
Our hearts and souls in love's sweet knot are bind.

PART III

The Depths of Desire

Velvet Nights

In velvet nights, where shadows softly creep,
Our bodies find a haven from the day,
In silken dark, where passions never sleep,
We lose ourselves in love's alluring sway.

Thy touch, a whisper on the tender skin,
A symphony of sighs and muted moans,
In velvet nights, our secret dreams begin,
A world where love and longing are intoned.

Each moment drips with honeyed, sweet desire,
In darkness deep, our souls do intertwine,
We dance amidst the shadows, hearts afire,
In velvet nights, where love's pure light does shine.

Thus, in the night, where velvet drapes the sky,
Our hearts are freed to love, to dream, to fly.

CHAPTER 12

Forbidden Longings

In hidden places, where the heart does dwell,
Lie yearnings kept in shadows, deep and dark,
Forbidden longings, which no words may tell,
A silent flame, an ever-burning spark.

Thy face, a vision haunting in my dreams,
A touch I crave but dare not seek to find,
In quiet moments, where the moonlight beams,
My heart is shackled, yet my thoughts unbind.

Oh, how I long for love that's out of reach,
A taste of paradise, forbidden sweet,
In every glance, a lesson love does teach,
Of passions fierce, and hearts that daring beat.

Thus, in the silence, where my secrets lie,
Forbidden longings rise, yet never die.

CHAPTER 13

Temptation's Call

In twilight's hush, where shadows gently fall,
A whisper soft, a siren's sweet entreat,
My soul is stirred by love's temptation call,
A melody of yearning, pure and fleet.

Thy voice, a song that dances through my mind,
In every note, a promise of delight,
With every word, our fates are thus entwined,
In temptation's call, we take our flight.

Oh, how the lure of passion's tender kiss,
Does beckon me to realms of wild desire,
In every touch, a prelude to our bliss,
As hearts and souls are set alight with fire.

Thus, in the dusk, where shadows softly sprawl,
We answer to love's sweet temptation call.

CHAPTER 14

Moonlit Rendezvous

Beneath the moon's soft gaze, our love does bloom,
A secret meeting bathed in silver light,
In moonlit rendezvous, we banish gloom,
And find our heaven in the starry night.

Thy eyes, a mirror to my longing soul,
In every glance, a promise pure and true,
In moonlit realms, where hearts do seek their goal,
Our love ignites, as fresh as morning dew.

Each moment shared beneath the lunar glow,
Is etched in time, a memory divine,
In every touch, a fervent love does show,
A bond that's written in the stars' own line.

Thus, in the night, where moonlit shadows lie,
Our hearts unite, beneath the endless sky.

CHAPTER 15

Eternal Flames

In passion's forge, where love's bright fire burns,
Our souls are melded, tempered by desire,
An endless blaze, that never fades or turns,
Eternal flames that lift our spirits higher.

Thy kiss, a spark that lights the darkest night,
In every touch, our love is set alight,
We dance in flames, where hearts and souls unite,
A fire that blazes ever pure and bright.

Oh, how the fire of passion's tender glow,
Does warm our hearts, in every sweet embrace,
In love's eternal flames, we come to know,
A paradise that time cannot erase.

Thus, in this fire, where love's bright embers play,
Our hearts are bound in flames that never sway.

PART IV

Trials of the Heart

CHAPTER 16

Stormy Seas

Upon the stormy seas, where tempests rage,
Our love is tested by the fierce winds' might,
Yet through the gale, we write our own love's page,
Our bond enduring through the darkest night.

Thy voice, a beacon in the howling storm,
Guides me to shores where calm and peace reside,
In turbulent waves, thy love keeps me warm,
A steady anchor when the seas are wide.

Though trials rise and waves crash all around,
Our hearts remain as one, steadfast and true,
In stormy seas, where challenges abound,
We find our strength in love's enduring view.

Thus, in the tempest, where the wild winds blow,
Our love prevails, and evermore does grow.

CHAPTER 17

Whispers of Doubt

In quiet moments, when the night is still,
The whispers of doubt creep into our hearts,
With shadows casting fears that chill,
We question if our love can mend the parts.

Thy face, a mirror of my own deep fears,
In every glance, uncertainty does rise,
Yet through the doubts, thy touch dries all my tears,
And brings me back to where our true love lies.

Oh, how the whispers try to tear us down,
To plant the seeds of worry and despair,
But love's pure light can never make us frown,
For in each other's arms, we find repair.

Thus, in the silence, where our fears are sown,
We vanquish doubt, and make our love our own.

CHAPTER 18

Love's Labyrinth

Within love's labyrinth, where paths entwine,
We wander lost, yet searching for our way,
With every twist and turn, our hearts align,
And find the strength to face another day.

Thy hand in mine, we navigate the maze,
In every step, a challenge we confront,
Through winding paths and unexpected days,
Our love's resilience bears the brunt.

Oh, how the journey tests our spirits' might,
In corridors of shadowed, twisting lanes,
Yet in thy eyes, I find my guiding light,
A beacon through the trials and the pains.

Thus, in love's labyrinth, where trials lay,
We find our way, and never go astray.

CHAPTER 19

Shattered Trust

When trust is shattered, like a broken glass,
The shards of doubt cut deep into the soul,
In painful echoes, memories amass,
And love seems distant, far beyond control.

Thy actions, once a balm to soothe my fears,
Now cast a shadow on our love's bright flame,
Yet through the tears, and in the passing years,
We seek to mend the heart and end the shame.

Oh, how the road to trust rebuilt is long,
A journey fraught with steps of faith and pain,
But in thy arms, I find where I belong,
A place where love can flourish once again.

Thus, in the aftermath of broken trust,
We rise anew, and heal the wounds we must.

CHAPTER 20

Hearts Repaired

Through trials faced and battles bravely fought,
Our love emerges stronger, pure, and bright,
In hearts repaired, the lessons we have sought,
Bring us together, shining in the night.

Thy touch, a healing balm upon my scars,
In every word, a promise to renew,
With time and care, we mend what once was marred,
And find our love grows deeper, ever true.

Oh, how the strength of love's enduring flame,
Can heal the wounds that time and trials bear,
In hearts repaired, we cast aside the blame,
And build a future filled with love and care.

Thus, in the journey where our trials lay,
Our hearts repaired, we find love's brighter day.

PART V

Sacred Union

CHAPTER 21

Vows Unbroken

In sacred vows we pledge our hearts to keep,
A promise made beneath the heavens' light,
In every word, a bond that's forged so deep,
A union blessed by stars and purest night.

Thy hand in mine, we walk this path as one,
In vows unbroken, steadfast through the years,
Our love a journey only just begun,
Through joy and sorrow, laughter, and the tears.

Oh, how the strength of vows can guide our way,
A compass true when tempests seek to bind,
In every promise, love's sweet light will stay,
A beacon clear, our hearts and souls combined.

Thus, in these vows, our love's bright flame does shine,
A sacred union, ever pure, divine.

CHAPTER 22

Sacred Bond

In quiet moments where our spirits meet,
We find a bond that words cannot express,
A sacred union, perfect and complete,
In every glance, a touch of tenderness.

Thy love, a force that binds my heart to thine,
In every breath, a whisper of our truth,
A sacred bond that neither time nor line
Can ever break, a testament to youth.

Oh, how our souls do dance in light's embrace,
A choreography of love and grace,
In sacred bond, we find our perfect place,
Where hearts and spirits join in endless space.

Thus, in this bond, our love's true strength is found,
A sacred union, pure and unbound.

CHAPTER 23

Eternal Embrace

In love's eternal embrace, we are entwined,
A dance of souls beneath the starlit sky,
In every touch, a world of dreams enshrined,
A timeless bond that time cannot deny.

Thy arms, a haven from life's stormy seas,
In every heartbeat, comfort's sweet refrain,
With love's embrace, we find our hearts at ease,
A sanctuary from all worldly pain.

Oh, how the strength of love's embrace can heal,
In tender moments, where our spirits soar,
In every touch, our hearts begin to feel
A deeper love that grows forevermore.

Thus, in this embrace, where time does cease,
We find our heaven, in love's sweet release.

CHAPTER 24

Union of Souls

In union of our souls, we find our home,
A place where love and spirit intertwine,
In every glance, a world where we can roam,
A bond so pure, it borders the divine.

Thy soul with mine, a melody so sweet,
A harmony that echoes through the night,
In union deep, our hearts and souls do meet,
Creating symphonies of pure delight.

Oh, how this union binds us ever tight,
A sacred bond that time can't erode,
In love's pure light, we find our endless night,
A journey shared, on love's eternal road.

Thus, in this union, where our souls are free,
We find our place, where love's pure light does be.

CHAPTER 25

Love's Sanctuary

In love's sanctuary, we find our peace,
A haven from the world's relentless storm,
In every touch, our worries find release,
A place where hearts and spirits are reborn.

Thy love, a shelter from life's wildest gale,
In every whisper, comfort's sweet embrace,
In love's pure haven, we will never fail,
For in each other's arms, we find our place.

Oh, how this sanctuary guards our hearts,
A fortress strong, where love and peace reside,
In every moment, where our love imparts
A sense of calm, where we can safely hide.

Thus, in this sanctuary, love does reign,
A sacred space, where hearts are freed from pain.

Love's Eternal Dance

CHAPTER 26

Timeless Waltz

In timeless waltz, where love's sweet rhythm flows,
We dance beneath the moon's enchanting light,
With every step, a harmony that grows,
Our hearts entwined, as day transforms to night.

Thy hand in mine, we glide across the floor,
In every movement, passion's flame does burn,
A dance that speaks of love forevermore,
In timeless waltz, our souls begin to yearn.

Oh, how the music of our hearts does play,
A symphony of love that never ends,
In every note, a promise to convey,
A dance where lovers join, where time suspends.

Thus, in this waltz, where love and time entwine,
We find eternity, in steps divine.

CHAPTER 27

Celestial Dance

Beneath the stars, where galaxies do spin,
Our love's celestial dance begins to play,
In cosmic waltz, where heaven's light shines in,
We find our place among the Milky Way.

Thy touch, a comet streaking through the night,
In every kiss, a burst of stellar fire,
In love's celestial dance, we take our flight,
Our hearts and souls ascending ever higher.

Oh, how the universe conspires in tune,
To guide our dance across the astral sea,
In every twirl, beneath the silver moon,
We find our love's eternal melody.

Thus, in the heavens, where the stars align,
We dance forever, in love's light divine.

CHAPTER 28

Eternal Tango

In love's eternal tango, fierce and bold,
Our bodies move as one, a perfect grace,
With every step, our story does unfold,
A dance of passion in a close embrace.

Thy gaze, a flame that sets my soul alight,
In every glance, a spark of wild desire,
In tango's dance, we lose ourselves in flight,
A whirlwind of emotion, burning fire.

Oh, how the tango's rhythm binds us tight,
In every beat, our hearts sync into one,
In love's eternal dance, both day and night,
We find our paradise, our rising sun.

Thus, in this tango, where our spirits meet,
We dance forever, in love's fervent heat.

CHAPTER 29

Moonlight Ballet

In moonlight ballet, where our shadows play,
We find a world where love's pure magic lies,
In every leap and twirl, our hearts convey
A symphony beneath the midnight skies.

Thy form, a silhouette against the moon,
In graceful arcs, we trace love's tender line,
In every pirouette, a love so soon
Transformed into a dance, a sign divine.

Oh, how the night does guide our every move,
A ballet where our souls are intertwined,
In moonlit dance, we find the path to prove
That love's eternal light is never blind.

Thus, in this ballet, where our spirits soar,
We dance in moonlight, love forevermore.

CHAPTER 30

Dance of Forever

In dance of forever, where time stands still,
Our love's eternal steps do light the way,
In every turn, a promise to fulfill,
A vow that carries us both night and day.

Thy hand in mine, we journey through the years,
In every dance, a new horizon found,
Through joy and sorrow, laughter, and the tears,
Our love's eternal dance knows no bound.

Oh, how this dance does guide us through our life,
A testament to love's unending grace,
In every moment, free from worldly strife,
We find our heaven in each other's face.

Thus, in this dance of forever, where we find
Our hearts and souls in perfect love entwined.

Seasons of Intimacy

CHAPTER 31

Spring's Embrace

In spring's embrace, where blossoms gently bloom,
Our love awakens with the morning dew,
In every bud, a promise to exhume,
A testament to passion pure and true.

Thy touch, a whisper on the budding leaves,
In every caress, life begins anew,
As flowers dance beneath the gentle breeze,
Our hearts entwine, our love's sweet rendezvous.

Oh, how the springtime breathes a tender sigh,
With every petal, love's fresh fragrance flows,
In nature's song, our spirits learn to fly,
A dance of hearts where love forever grows.

Thus, in the spring, where intimacy reigns,
Our love is reborn, free from past's old chains.

CHAPTER 32

Summer's Heat

In summer's heat, where passion's fire burns bright,
Our love ignites beneath the blazing sun,
In every touch, a spark of pure delight,
As two become a fusion, merged as one.

Thy kiss, a flame that sears my willing soul,
In every breath, a promise fierce and bold,
In summer's heat, our hearts have found their goal,
A love that's timeless, never growing old.

Oh, how the days stretch long, with light and fire,
A season where our souls in heat collide,
In every moment, burning with desire,
Our love's intensity cannot be denied.

Thus, in the summer, where the flames run high,
Our hearts are bound beneath the fiery sky.

CHAPTER 33

Autumn's Whisper

In autumn's whisper, where the leaves do fall,
Our love matures, in shades of red and gold,
In every breeze, we hear the season's call,
A tale of passion that's been gently told.

Thy hand in mine, we walk through fields of change,
In every step, a memory is born,
As nature shifts, our love does rearrange,
A dance of hearts that time cannot forlorn.

Oh, how the autumn's chill does weave its spell,
In every rustle, secrets of the heart,
In whispers soft, where love and longing dwell,
We find our solace, never to depart.

Thus, in the autumn, where the world transforms,
Our love endures, through all life's varied storms.

CHAPTER 34

Winter's Warmth

In winter's warmth, where snow lies pure and white,
Our love finds shelter from the cold outside,
In every embrace, we hold each other tight,
A sanctuary where our hearts reside.

Thy touch, a warmth against the icy chill,
In every glance, a fire that softly glows,
In winter's depth, our love does thus fulfill,
A promise kept as gently as the snows.

Oh, how the season's quiet brings us near,
In every silence, love's sweet voice is heard,
In winter's peace, we find a love sincere,
A whispered vow in every softly spoken word.

Thus, in the winter, where the world is still,
Our love remains, a beacon of pure will.

CHAPTER 35

Seasons' Cycle

In seasons' cycle, where our love does flow,
We find a rhythm that's both new and old,
In every change, our hearts begin to grow,
A story of intimacy retold.

Thy love, a constant through the shifting times,
In every season, passion's steady beat,
Through spring's sweet blooms and summer's heated climbs,
Our love's eternal dance is ever sweet.

Oh, how the autumn's hues and winter's white,
Do paint our love with colors rich and deep,
In every season, whether day or night,
We find a bond that time and trials keep.

Thus, in the cycle, where the seasons blend,
Our love endures, a journey with no end.

PART VIII

Love's Eternal Echo

CHAPTER 36

Whispered Memories

In whispered memories of days gone by,
Our love's eternal echo softly plays,
A symphony that never says goodbye,
But lingers in the heart through all the days.

Thy voice, a melody that haunts my dreams,
In every note, a memory divine,
In whispered tones, our love's pure essence gleams,
A timeless song that weaves your heart with mine.

Oh, how the echoes carry through the years,
A gentle reminder of our shared past,
In every whisper, vanishing all fears,
A love that's boundless, infinite, and vast.

Thus, in the echoes of our whispered song,
Our love's sweet memory forever strong.

CHAPTER 37

Timeless Reverie

In timeless reverie, where dreams reside,
Our love's eternal echo finds its place,
In every thought, where fantasies abide,
We see the shadows of our love's embrace.

Thy image, like a beacon in the night,
Guides me through realms where time does not constrain,
In dreams, our love is always pure and bright,
A perfect union, free from earthly pain.

Oh, how the reverie sustains my soul,
A refuge where our spirits meet and blend,
In timeless dreams, our hearts remain whole,
A love that echoes to the very end.

Thus, in these reveries, where time stands still,
Our love's sweet echo does my heart fulfill.

CHAPTER 38

Echoes of the Heart

In echoes of the heart, where love does sing,
A chorus of our memories so clear,
Each beat a testament to everything
That binds us close, dispelling every fear.

Thy laughter, like a songbird's gentle call,
Resounds within my heart's most sacred space,
In echoes true, I feel our love enthrall,
A melody that time cannot erase.

Oh, how the echoes bring us back in time,
To moments filled with joy and pure delight,
In every beat, our hearts in rhythm rhyme,
A love that shines in darkest of the night.

Thus, in these echoes, where our hearts align,
Our love endures, a song forever mine.

CHAPTER 39

Eternal Reflection

In eternal reflection, where love's light
Is mirrored in the depths of memory's glass,
We see the moments pure and shining bright,
A legacy that time can never pass.

Thy smile, a beacon in the mirrored past,
Reflects the joy we shared in days of old,
In every glance, a love that's built to last,
A story in reflections softly told.

Oh, how the mirror holds our love's sweet tale,
A timeless portrait framed in heart's embrace,
In every gaze, our love does thus prevail,
A testament to time's enduring grace.

Thus, in reflection, where our love is shown,
Our hearts are bound, eternally our own.

CHAPTER 40

Forever's Echo

In forever's echo, where love's sound
Reverberates through time and endless space,
Our souls in harmony are ever bound,
A symphony that nothing can erase.

Thy love, a constant echo in my mind,
Resounds through ages, strong and ever clear,
In every moment, there our hearts do find
A love that's timeless, never to disappear.

Oh, how the echoes carry through the years,
A gentle chorus of our shared refrain,
In forever's echo, vanish all our fears,
A love that's endless, free from earthly pain.

Thus, in these echoes, where our love does lie,
Our hearts and souls in harmony do sigh.

PART IX

The Ephemeral and the Eternal

CHAPTER 41

Fleeting Moments

In fleeting moments, where our love does bloom,
A fragile beauty dances in the light,
Ephemeral as spring's first fragrant plume,
Yet lasting in the heart through day and night.

Thy touch, a whisper on the morning breeze,
A transient joy that fills my soul with grace,
In every glance, a memory to seize,
A love that time and space cannot erase.

Oh, how these moments, though they swiftly fade,
Leave echoes that resound within our hearts,
A fleeting joy that time cannot invade,
A bond that from our souls will not depart.

Thus, in these fleeting moments, pure and rare,
Our love's eternal truth is always there.

CHAPTER 42

Eternal Flame

Within the heart, an eternal flame does burn,
A light that guides us through life's darkest hours,
In every trial, to this love we return,
A beacon shining through the fiercest showers.

Thy love, a fire that never dims or dies,
In every heartbeat, warmth and comfort flows,
An endless flame that lights up midnight skies,
And in its glow, our love forever grows.

Oh, how the flame of love does brightly shine,
Through storms and calm, a constant, guiding light,
In every spark, a promise so divine,
A love that burns eternal, pure, and bright.

Thus, in this flame, where heart and soul do meet,
We find our love, eternal and complete.

CHAPTER 43

Passing Shadows

In passing shadows, where our fears reside,
We find the strength to face the unknown night,
With love's eternal flame as our true guide,
We banish darkness with a single light.

Thy courage, like a star that pierces through,
The deepest shadows, casting them aside,
In every moment, love does thus renew,
A bond that even shadows cannot hide.

Oh, how the shadows flee before love's glow,
A fleeting darkness in the light of day,
In every touch, our hearts and spirits grow,
And find a path where love will always stay.

Thus, in these shadows, where our fears may roam,
Our love shines bright, and guides us safely home.

CHAPTER 44

Timeless Love

In timeless love, where moments blend and fade,
We find a truth that nothing can obscure,
A bond that's forged in light and never swayed,
A love that stands eternal, strong, and pure.

Thy heart, a constant beat that guides my own,
In every breath, a promise to endure,
Through all of life, no matter how unknown,
A love that's timeless, steadfast, and secure.

Oh, how the sands of time may shift and change,
Yet in our hearts, a love that's ever true,
In every moment, we do thus arrange,
A tapestry of life that's bright and new.

Thus, in this love, where time does intertwine,
Our hearts are bound in rhythms so divine.

Eternal Echo

In eternal echo, where our love resounds,
A symphony of hearts in perfect tune,
In every beat, a joy that knows no bounds,
A melody that rises with the moon.

Thy voice, an echo in the still of night,
A whisper that enshrines our deepest dreams,
In every note, a promise of delight,
A love that echoes through life's winding streams.

Oh, how the echoes carry through the years,
A timeless chorus of our shared refrain,
In eternal echo, vanish all our fears,
A love that's endless, free from earthly pain.

Thus, in these echoes, where our love does lie,
Our hearts and souls in harmony do sigh.

Reflections and Reveries

Mirror of the Heart

In the mirror of the heart, we see our truth,
A reflection of the love we hold so dear,
In every glance, a vision of our youth,
A memory that time cannot make sear.

Thy eyes, a portal to our shared past,
Reflecting joys and sorrows intertwined,
In every look, a love that's built to last,
A bond that time and trials cannot bind.

Oh, how the mirror shows us what we've gained,
A life of love, with memories so bright,
In every reflection, nothing is feigned,
Our hearts connected, glowing in the light.

Thus, in this mirror, where our souls are shown,
We see our love, eternal and our own.

CHAPTER 47

Dreams of Yesterday

In dreams of yesterday, our love does live,
A reverie where time does not exist,
In every dream, a memory we give,
A kiss that lingers, a tender tryst.

Thy touch, a whisper in the dream's soft light,
A caress that spans both time and space,
In every dream, our hearts take flight,
A journey to a secret, sacred place.

Oh, how these dreams sustain our hearts each day,
A sanctuary where our love is pure,
In reveries, where shadows fade away,
We find a bond that time cannot obscure.

Thus, in these dreams, where memories reside,
Our love remains, forever side by side.

CHAPTER 48

Reflections in the Moonlight

In reflections in the moonlight's gentle glow,
Our love's sweet reveries softly arise,
In every beam, a tender tale does show,
A story written in the night skies.

Thy face, illuminated by the moon,
In every glance, a memory takes flight,
In reflections, where love's sweet song is strewn,
We find a world of pure and soft delight.

Oh, how the moonlight casts its silver hue,
Upon the path our hearts and souls have walked,
In every shadow, love's reflection true,
A silent conversation, softly talked.

Thus, in the moonlight, where reflections play,
Our love's sweet reveries forever stay.

CHAPTER 49

Reverie of the Stars

In the reverie of stars, we find our dream,
A celestial dance of hearts aligned,
In every twinkle, love's eternal gleam,
A constellation of our souls combined.

Thy love, a star that guides me through the night,
In every spark, a promise to endure,
In reveries where stars' pure light burns bright,
We find a love that's timeless, true, and sure.

Oh, how the heavens speak of our sweet bond,
A tapestry of stars that shine above,
In every star, a memory is spawned,
A testament to our unending love.

Thus, in the stars, where reveries reside,
Our love's eternal light does never hide.

CHAPTER 50

Reflections of Forever

In reflections of forever, love does gleam,
A timeless echo in the heart's pure core,
In every moment, a shared, endless dream,
A journey that will last forevermore.

Thy love, a mirror of my soul's desire,
In every glance, a world of wonder found,
In reflections, where our hearts conspire,
We find a love that's pure, and so profound.

Oh, how the reflections show our path,
A journey where our spirits intertwine,
In every look, a love that always lasts,
A bond that's sacred, beautiful, divine.

Thus, in forever's mirror, we do see,
Our love's eternal reverie, pure and free.

In the quiet moments, when the world is still, and the whispers of the heart are the only sound, we find the essence of our journey through love and intimacy. Each poem, a testament to the phases of our shared existence, has woven a tapestry of passion, trials, and eternal echoes that define what it means to love deeply and truly. Our hearts, bound by these words, have traversed the seasons and cycles of love, finding in each reflection a new depth of connection.

Through fleeting moments and enduring flames, our love has been a constant, a guiding star that illuminates the darkest nights and the brightest days. We have danced through the reveries and faced the shadows, always returning to the light of our shared bond. This collection is not just a series of poems, but a chronicle of the love that lives within us, a love that transcends time and space.

As we turn the final page, let us carry these reflections with us, for in them lies the truth of our journey. Love, in all its forms, is an eternal dance, a timeless reverie that echoes through the corridors of our hearts, whispering promises of forever.

Afterword: The Enduring Power of Love and Intimacy

Love and intimacy are the bedrock upon which our lives are built. They are the forces that drive us to connect, to share, and to create memories that transcend the mundane and touch the divine. Throughout the ages, love has been the muse for countless poets, the inspiration for artists, and the motivation for dreamers. It is in these connections, these moments of pure, unfiltered emotion, that we find the essence of what it means to be human.

The poems in this collection have explored the many facets of love—from its awakening to its trials, from the ephemeral to the eternal. They have shown us that love is not a single moment, but a series of experiences that shape our souls and define our lives. It is a journey that takes us through the seasons of intimacy, guiding us with its light and comforting us with its warmth.

In love, we find not only joy but also strength. It is in the arms of a beloved that we find solace from the world's chaos, and it is in their eyes that we see the reflection of our best selves. Love, in its purest form, is an enduring force, a timeless connection that binds us across the expanse of time.

As you close this book, may you carry with you the echoes of its verses and the reveries of its lines. Let them be a reminder that love, in all its forms, is eternal. It is the whisper in the wind, the star in the night sky, and the beat in our hearts. It is the thread that weaves our lives together, creating a tapestry of experiences that define who we are and what we hold dear.

May your journey through love be as profound and enduring as the words within these pages, and may you always find the beauty in the fleeting and the eternal, the ephemeral and the everlasting.

Notes on Shakespearean Style

William Shakespeare, the renowned playwright and poet of the Elizabethan era, is celebrated for his masterful use of language, intricate poetic forms, and profound exploration of human emotion. The poems in this collection draw inspiration from Shakespeare's style, blending his classic techniques with modern English to create a timeless and accessible tribute to the Bard's genius.

1. Iambic Pentameter

One of the hallmarks of Shakespeare's verse is iambic pentameter, a metrical pattern that consists of five iambic feet per line. Each foot contains an unstressed syllable followed by a stressed syllable, creating a rhythmic flow that mimics natural speech. This collection maintains this meter to evoke the musicality and rhythm that define Shakespearean poetry.

1. Sonnets and Rhymed Couplets

Shakespeare's sonnets and rhymed couplets often feature intricate rhyme schemes and structured forms. The sonnets in this collection follow the traditional Shakespearean form, with three quatrains followed by a rhymed couplet (ABABCDCDEFEFGG). The use of rhymed couplets at the end of sonnets and other poems provides a sense of closure and emphasis.

1. Imagery and Metaphor

Vivid imagery and rich metaphors are central to Shakespeare's work, painting pictures with words and evoking deep emotional responses. The poems in this collection employ similar techniques, using nature, celestial bodies, and timeless themes to explore the complexities of love and intimacy.

1. Archaic Language and Diction

While these poems are written in modern English, they retain some archaic terms and phrases to capture the essence of Shakespeare's era. This blend of old and new language helps to create a bridge between the past and present, making the themes of love and passion universally resonant.

1. Emotional Depth and Exploration of Themes

Shakespeare's poetry delves into the depths of human emotion, exploring themes of love, desire, loss, and eternity. This collection mirrors these explorations, presenting love not just as a single emotion, but as a multifaceted experience that evolves and endures through life's various stages.

By combining these elements, the poems in this collection pay homage to Shakespeare's timeless style while making it accessible to contemporary readers. The result is a fusion of classic and modern, celebrating the enduring power of love through the lens of one of history's greatest poets.

1. **Anon**

Definition: Soon; shortly.
Example: "I will return anon."

1. **Betwixt**

Definition: Between.
Example: "Betwixt the stars and moon."

1. **Comet**

Definition: A celestial body moving in space, often with a glowing tail.
Example: "Thy touch, a comet streaking through the night."

1. **Doth**

Definition: Does.
Example: "How doth thy heart beat so?"

1. **Ephemeral**

Definition: Lasting for a very short time.
Example: "Ephemeral as spring's first fragrant plume."

1. **Forsooth**

Definition: Indeed; truly.
Example: "Forsooth, our love endures."

1. **Hark**

Definition: Listen.
Example: "Hark, the echoes of our hearts."

1. **Hath**

Definition: Has.
Example: "Love hath no end."

1. **Intertwine**

Definition: Twist or twine together.
Example: "Our hearts and souls do intertwine."

1. **Milky Way**

Definition: The galaxy containing our solar system, often visible as a band of light in the night sky.

Example: "We find our place among the Milky Way."

1. Naught

Definition: Nothing.
Example: "Love endures, when naught else does."

1. O'er

Definition: Over.
Example: "O'er the moonlit path."

1. Quoth

Definition: Said (used especially in literary or humorous contexts).
Example: "Quoth the poet in love's refrain."

1. Thy

Definition: Your (possessive form of thou).
Example: "Thy love, a constant star."

1. Twixt

Definition: Between.
Example: "Twixt dawn and dusk."

1. Verily

Definition: Truly; certainly.
Example: "Verily, our love is pure."

1. **Whence**

Definition: From where.
Example: "Whence comes this love so deep?"

1. **Yonder**

Definition: At some distance in the direction indicated; over there.
Example: "Yonder stars that light our way."

This glossary provides definitions for terms that evoke the spirit of Shakespearean language, enhancing the reader's appreciation of the timeless quality of the poems.

Joel Hawksley is a distinguished US Army veteran, having served as a Paratrooper, Military Policeman, and Communication Specialist during both peacetime and combat. With 37 years of marriage, he and his ex-wife raised three children, Joshua, Grace, and Adam, and he is the proud grandfather of Rain and Emma.

Joel's diverse career spans retail, sales, education, and politics, culminating in the co-founding of J & Washington with David Washington. Despite facing numerous challenges and adversities, Joel's dedication to writing has remained a constant source of strength and expression throughout his life.

As an author, Joel has penned four notable books: "Bringing America Together Again," "Presidential Chronicles," "When Serpents Shed Their Skins," and "The Weight of Existence." Today, he continues to share his poetry and prose with the world, enriching readers with his insightful and heartfelt works.